Animals and the Environment
Snakes

Copperheads

by Linda George

Content Consultants:

Donal M. Boyer
Associate Curator
Reptile Department
San Diego Zoo

"Bayou" Bob Popplewell
Brazos Snake Ranch
Santo, Texas

CAPSTONE
HIGH/LOW BOOKS
an imprint of Capstone Press

CAPSTONE PRESS

818 North Willow Street • Mankato, Minnesota 56001
http://www.capstone-press.com

Library of Congress Cataloging-in-Publication Data
George, Linda.
   Copperheads/by Linda George.
   p. cm.--(Animals and the environment)
   Includes bibliographical references (p.45) and index.
   Summary: Describes the physical characteristics, habitat, and behavior
of copperhead snakes.
   ISBN 1-56065-693-X
   1. Copperheads--Juvenile literature. [1. Copperhead. 2. Poisonous
snakes. 3. Snakes.] I. Title. II. Series: Animals & the environment.
QL666.O69G463   1998
597.96--dc21

                                        97-31674
                                           CIP
                                            AC

Editorial credits
Editor, Matt Doeden; cover design, Timothy Halldin; illustrations,
   James Franklin; photo research, Michelle L. Norstad

Photo credits
Thomas R. Fletcher, 11
James P. Rowan, 19
Leonard Lee Rue III, 31, 34
Allen Blake Sheldon, cover
Unicorn Stock Photos/Russell R. Grundke, 12; Robert W. Ginn, 41
Visuals Unlimited/Joe McDonald, 6, 25, 29, 38, 42; Gary W. Carter, 8;
   Milton H. Tierney Jr., 14; Parke H. John Jr., 17; Jim Merli, 21, 22, 26,
   32, 36

Table of Contents

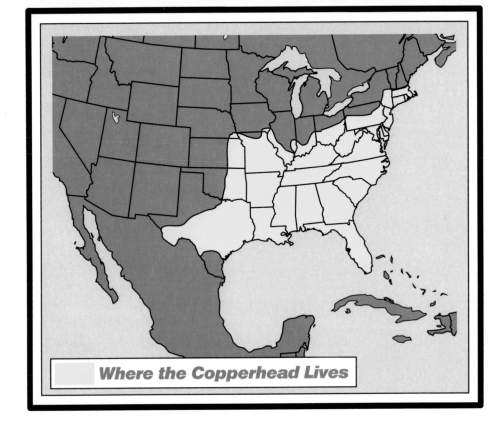

Where the Copperhead Lives

Fast Facts about Copperheads

Kinds: There are four main kinds of copperheads. All copperheads are in the family Viperidae. A family is a group of related animals.

Description: Copperheads are usually 20 to 36 inches (51 to 91 centimeters) long. Their bodies are thick and heavy. Most copperheads are reddish-brown. Copperheads have bands of color that wrap

4

around their bodies. The bands are narrow on the snake's top and bottom and thick on the sides. They are shaped like hourglasses.

Habits: Copperheads bite to defend themselves and while they are hunting. Copperheads only bite people if the snakes are surprised.

Food: Copperheads eat small animals like rats and mice. They also eat lizards, frogs, and large insects.

Reproduction: Copperheads mate during spring. Female copperheads have four to eight young during summer.

Life span: Copperheads live about 20 years.

Habitat: Copperheads live in woodlands and on rocky hillsides near water. Some spend time on the edges of swamps.

Range: Copperheads live mostly in the eastern and southern United States.

Chapter 1
About Copperheads

Copperheads are pit vipers. Pit vipers have loreal pits on their heads. Loreal pits are small holes near some snakes' eyes. Snakes use these pits to sense other animals' body heat.

Copperheads and other pit vipers are venomous. They inject venom when they bite. Venom is a poisonous liquid produced by some animals.

Copperheads are pit vipers.

Copperheads have flat, triangle-shaped heads. The tops of their heads are copper colored. They are the same color as a new penny. This color gives copperheads their name.

Copperheads have thick, reddish-brown bodies. Some copperheads have brown bands that wrap around their bodies. The bands are narrow on the snake's top and bottom and thick on the sides. The bands are shaped like hourglasses.

Where Copperheads Live

Most copperheads live in open woodlands or on rocky hillsides. They stay near streams, lakes, ponds, and swamps. Some copperheads live in trash piles and old buildings. Others live under rocks and rotten logs. Copperheads live where there are plenty of hiding places.

Many copperheads live in thick plant growth along a river called the Rio Grande. The Rio Grande runs between Texas and Mexico.

Copperheads live where there are plenty of hiding places.

Copperheads need places to lie in the sun on cool days. They must lie in the sun to keep warm. All snakes are cold-blooded. This means the temperature of their bodies changes depending on the weather. In cold weather, their bodies cool down. In warm weather, their bodies heat up.

In late fall, copperheads join other copperheads in dens. The snakes hibernate during winter. Hibernate means to spend the winter in a deep sleep.

In spring and fall, copperheads spend their days in warm, sunny places. This keeps their bodies warm. During summer, copperheads come out mostly at night. The daytime sun is often too hot for them.

Copperhead Senses

Copperheads see better at night than many snakes. The pupil of a copperhead's eye is a thin slit, like a cat's. A pupil is the black part of an eyeball that lets in light. Most snakes that are not venomous have round pupils.

Loreal pits help copperheads hunt at night.

Copperheads' pupils give them better night vision than many other snakes. Slitted pupils gather more light than round pupils.

Loreal pits also help copperheads find prey at night. Prey is an animal hunted by another animal for food.

Copperheads cannot hear because they do not have eardrums. But copperheads can feel vibrations in the ground. Vibrations are movements of the ground caused by moving

Copperheads flick their tongues out every few seconds to smell and taste the air.

animals. Some scientists think copperheads use their ability to sense vibrations the way other animals use hearing.

Copperheads sense mainly through smell and taste. They flick their forked tongues out every few seconds to smell and taste the air. Their tongues sample the air around them.

Copperheads rub their tongues against their Jacobson's organs. The Jacobson's organs are tiny sacs at the top of copperheads' mouths. They are special taste and odor detectors.

Molting

A copperhead has several layers of skin. One layer is the snake's scales. Another gives the copperhead its colors. Copperheads also have a clear outer layer of skin.

Like all snakes, copperheads molt. Molt means to shed an outer layer of skin. Copperheads grow a new layer of outer skin while they molt. The skin over a molting snake's eyes turns white. Soon, the skin begins to peel away from the mouth. The snake wiggles out of the peeling skin and leaves it behind. The snake already has a new layer of outer skin. Copperhead colors and markings are especially bright right after the snakes molt.

Chapter 2

Kinds of Copperheads

There are four main kinds of copperheads. They are the northern, southern, broad-banded, and trans-Pecos copperheads. All true copperheads live in North America.

Some other snakes look like copperheads. They have similar markings. But these snakes do not live in North America.

The northern copperhead is one of four main kinds of copperheads.

Northern Copperheads

Northern copperheads live in the eastern United States. They usually stay in hilly areas. Sometimes northern copperheads move to fields of grain during the summer. They hunt for prey in the fields.

Most adult northern copperheads are 24 to 36 inches (61 to 91 centimeters) long. They usually have light brown bodies. Some are pink. Dark reddish-brown bands wrap around their bodies.

Northern copperheads are camouflaged. Camouflage is coloring that makes an animal look like its surroundings. Camouflage helps northern copperheads hunt prey without being seen.

Young northern copperheads are about eight inches (20 centimeters) long when they are born. They are more brightly colored than adults. They have yellow or green tails. They use their tails to bring in prey. Small animals

Northern copperheads are camouflaged.

sometimes mistake the tails for worms. A young copperhead attacks if prey comes close.

Some people think northern copperheads smell like cucumbers. A cucumber is a long, green vegetable. The snake's odor is really copperhead musk. Musk is an oil that northern copperheads produce when they sense danger. Most predators will not eat copperheads when they smell like musk. A predator is an animal that hunts and eats other animals.

Southern Copperheads

Southern copperheads live mainly in the southeastern United States. Some live as far north as Illinois. Other names for southern copperheads include chunk heads, pilot snakes, poplar leaf snakes, and oak snakes.

Southern copperheads are paler and pinker than northern copperheads. They have pale pink or brown bands that wrap around their bodies.

Most adult southern copperheads are 24 to 36 inches (61 to 91 centimeters) long. They

**Southern copperheads are paler than
northern copperheads.**

live near swamps and streams bordered by
trees. They also live in hilly areas.

Southern copperheads sometimes make
noises with their tails like rattlesnakes. But
they do not have rattles. Southern
copperheads shake their tails across rocks or
dry leaves. This makes a sound similar to a
rattlesnake's rattle.

Broad-Banded Copperheads

Broad-banded copperheads live mostly in Oklahoma and Texas. These copperheads have wide, copper-brown bands on their bodies.

Broad-banded copperheads live in meadows and wooded areas. Some live near people. Many broad-banded copperheads make homes under piles of oak leaves. These leaves camouflage the snakes.

Most adult broad-banded copperheads are 20 to 30 inches (51 to 76 centimeters) long. Young broad-banded copperheads are seven to 10 inches (18 to 25 centimeters) long. They are usually paler than their parents.

Broad-banded copperheads maintain their body temperatures by lying in the sun during the day. They hide beneath leaves and branches in the morning and evening to stay warm. During summer, they often stay in shaded areas to avoid the hot sun. They also hunt at night during summer.

Broad-banded copperheads have wide bands on their bodies.

Trans-Pecos Copperheads

Trans-Pecos copperheads live in western Texas. They live in canyons and near water. They often make their homes in thick plant growth.

Most trans-Pecos copperheads are 20 to 30 inches (51 to 76 centimeters) long. The longest one ever found was almost three feet (91 centimeters) long.

Trans-Pecos copperheads are different shades of brown. Some are tan. Others are dark brown. Trans-Pecos copperheads have dark bands on their bodies. The bands become paler on the undersides of their bodies.

Trans-Pecos copperheads have spotted patterns on their undersides. They also have streaks of color. No other copperheads have these patterns. The spots are usually red, brown, or black. The tails of trans-Pecos copperheads are gray-brown with thin white bands.

Trans-Pecos copperheads live in western Texas.

Copperhead Look-Alikes

Some snakes look and act like copperheads. They also have deadly venom like true copperheads. These snakes live outside of North America. They live in parts of Australia and Asia. The only true copperheads live in North America.

Australian copperheads look different than true copperheads. But their heads are copper-colored like true copperheads. Some Australian copperheads are entirely black. They do not have slits for pupils like true copperheads. The pupils in their eyes are round. Australian copperheads move slowly. They rarely bite unless people step on them or pick them up.

All true copperheads live in North America.

Chapter 3
Hunting and Defense

Copperheads usually hunt at night. Their loreal pits make them excellent night hunters. Their prey includes small animals like rats and mice. They also eat birds, frogs, and large insects.

Copperheads have deadly venom. Their venom can kill small animals. It can also kill children. But copperhead venom rarely kills adults.

Copperheads hunt small animals like frogs.

Hunting Prey

Copperheads use their camouflage when hunting. They hide under leaves or rocks. They wait until prey comes near before attacking. They sense prey with their loreal pits. They also feel vibrations on the ground.

When copperheads bite, they inject venom through their fangs. A fang is a long, sharp tooth. Fangs are hollow. This allows venom to pass through them.

Copperheads bite quickly, then move away. They wait for the venom to slow their prey. Many other venomous snakes hold prey with their fangs and inject as much venom as they can.

Copperhead venom weakens blood vessels. It causes victims to bleed inside their bodies. It makes breathing difficult. Venom also makes victims lose control of some muscles.

Swallowing Food

Copperheads swallow prey whole. Sometimes the animals they eat are still alive. Copperheads

Copperheads swallow prey whole.

usually swallow prey headfirst. Copperheads
can swallow animals twice the size of their own
heads. The bones in copperhead jaws can
open wide. This allows copperheads to eat
large prey.

Swallowing takes a long time. A
copperhead's muscles slowly pull prey into
its body. The copperhead's teeth grasp the

prey's head. The prey often struggles while it is swallowed. Sometimes the prey does not die until after the copperhead has swallowed it.

Copperhead Strikes

Copperheads do not bite people unless they are surprised or sense danger. Most copperheads try to escape before biting a person. If a copperhead cannot escape, it may strike. Strike means to wound by biting. After a copperhead strikes, it usually tries again to escape.

Copperheads bite more people than rattlesnakes do. Copperhead venom makes most people very sick. But few people die from copperhead bites. Small children are the most likely to die.

Treating Copperhead Bites

Copperhead bites can be treated with an antivenin. An antivenin is a medicine that reduces the effects of venom. The victim of a copperhead bite must see a doctor immediately. The doctor can provide a shot of antivenin. Copperhead antivenin is made from chemicals in the snake's venom.

A scientist hooks a copperhead's fangs over the edge of a jar to collect venom.

Scientists collect venom to make antivenin. Collecting venom from a copperhead is dangerous. A scientist holds a copperhead by its neck. The copperhead may try to bite. The scientist hooks the copperhead's fangs over the edge of a jar. Venom comes out of the fangs and drips into the jar. Scientists call this milking a snake.

Chapter 4
Mating

Copperheads usually mate in spring. They perform special rituals before mating. A ritual is a set of actions that is always performed the same way.

Copperhead females give birth to young during the summer. They give birth about four months after mating.

Mating Rituals

Before mating, a male copperhead performs a series of movements. The male begins by

Young copperheads are born during summer.

touching the female with his nose. He places his head and neck on the female's back. Then he rubs the bottom of his mouth on her back. He slides his body against hers. Then he puts his tail next to the female's tail.

A female copperhead also performs a ritual before mating. She begins by crawling slowly forward. Then she stops. She waves her tail from side to side. Then she whips it back and forth. She flattens herself out and pushes waste from her body.

Then the copperheads mate. The male does not move. He remains still. The female raises her head and flicks her tongue. She moves her body over the male's. After mating, the male slithers away.

Young Copperheads

Female copperheads do not lay eggs like some snakes do. Instead, young copperheads grow in soft eggs that stay inside their

Young copperheads grow in soft eggs inside their mothers' bodies.

mothers' bodies. After about four months, female copperheads give birth to a brood of live young. A brood is a group of young animals born at the same time. The young copperheads are still in the soft eggs. They immediately push out of the eggs.

Female copperheads give birth in July, August, or September. They usually have four to eight young. Young copperheads are seven to 10 inches (18 to 25 centimeters) long. About twice as many male copperheads are born as females. Scientists are not sure why so many males are born.

A female copperhead does not stay with her young. The young are on their own within several minutes after they are born.

Newborn copperheads are already venomous enough to kill prey. They know how to hunt and kill. Some young copperheads know how to bring in prey with their colored tails.

Young copperheads bring in prey with their colored tails.

Chapter 5

Copperheads and People

Copperheads hurt people when they strike. Some people die from copperhead bites. But copperheads also help people. Copperheads eat rats, mice, and insects. These animals destroy crops. By eating these animals, copperheads help protect the food supply.

Meeting a Copperhead

Copperheads are usually quiet. They are often camouflaged and hard to see. It is easy to walk

Copperheads help protect crops by eating rats and mice.

near a copperhead without knowing it is there. A copperhead may strike if a person comes near.

People should be careful when walking in copperhead territory. They should wear boots and loose pants. The boots and loose pants could keep a copperhead's fangs from touching a person's skin.

People should stand still if they meet a copperhead. Sudden movements can frighten the snake. The best way to move away from a copperhead is to back up slowly.

The Future of Copperheads

People have moved into some of the copperhead's range. There are fewer natural places for copperheads to live. This means copperheads and humans live closer together than before.

Some people hunt and kill copperheads to display the snakes' skins. But copperheads are not in danger of becoming extinct. Extinct means no longer living anywhere on Earth. Instead, copperheads remain one of the most common snakes in North America.

There are fewer natural places for copperheads to live.

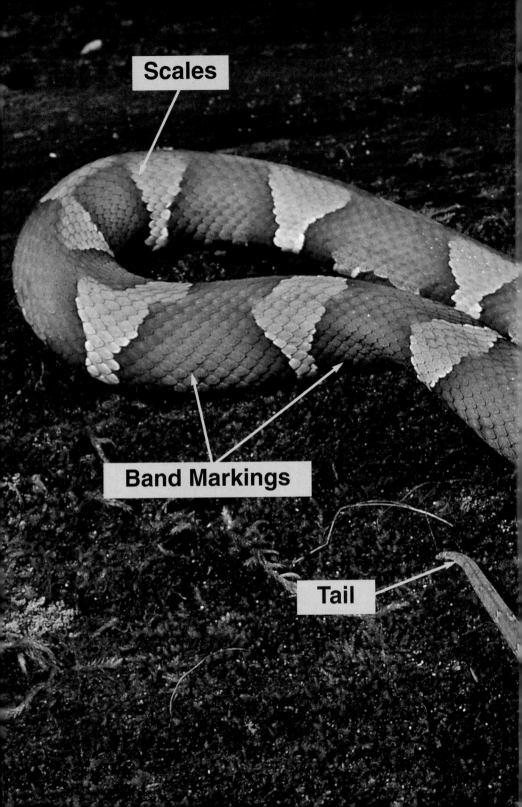

Scales

Band Markings

Tail

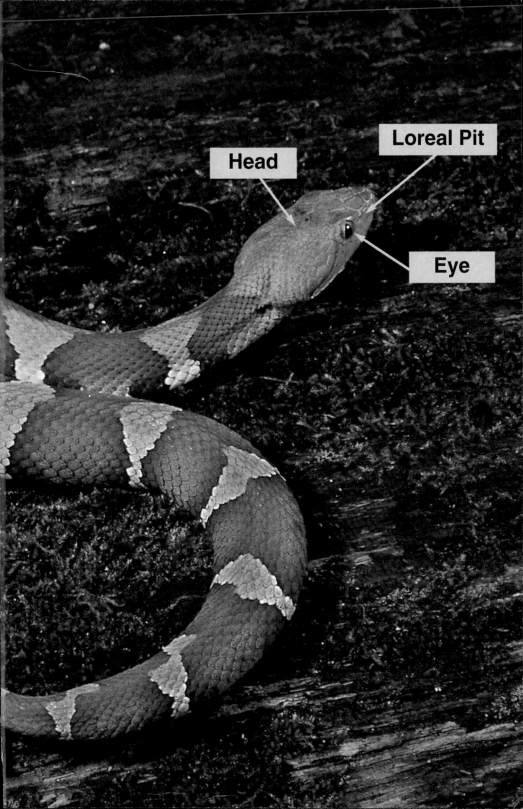

Words to Know

antivenin (an-ti-VEN-in)—a medicine that reduces the effects of snake poison

brood (BROOD)—a group of young animals born at the same time

camouflage (KAM-uh-flahzh)—coloring that makes an animal look like its surroundings

extinct (ek-STINGKT)—no longer living anywhere on Earth

fang (FANG)—a long, sharp tooth; venom passes through it.

musk (MUHSK)—an oil some snakes produce when they sense danger

predator (PRED-uh-tur)—an animal that hunts other animals for food

prey (PRAY)—an animal hunted by another animal for food

ritual (RICH-oo-uhl)—a set of actions that is always performed the same way

venom (VEN-uhm)—a poisonous liquid produced by some animals

To Learn More

Ethan, Eric. *Copperheads*. Milwaukee: Gareth Stevens, 1995.

Gerholdt, James E. *Copperheads*. Edina, Minn.: Abdo & Daughters, 1996.

Markle, Sandra. *Outside and Inside Snakes*. New York: Macmillan Books for Young Readers, 1995.

Stone, Lynn M. *Poison Fangs*. Vero Beach, Fla.: Rourke Press, 1996.

Useful Addresses

Fort Worth Zoo
1989 Colonial Parkway
Fort Worth, TX 76110-6640

Metropolitan Toronto Zoo
West Hill
Box 280
Toronto, ON M1D 4R5
Canada

National Zoological Park
3001 Connecticut Avenue NW
Washington, DC 20008

**Society for the Study of Amphibians and
  Reptiles**
P.O. Box 626
Hays, KS 67601-0626

Internet Sites

Broadbanded Copperhead
http://www.wf.net/~snake/copperhe.htm

Florida Gators, Snakes, Animals and Critters
http://www.gate.net/~critter1/critter/critter3.htm

Learn about Snakes!
http://www.mvhs.srvusd.k12.ca.us/~shayati/
    think.html

The Snake Page
http://www.geocities.com/CapeCanaveral/4538/

Index